Digital Lipstick on a Legacy Pig !

Digital Lipstick on a Legacy Pig!

A Practitioner's Personal Notes on Digital Transformation

Vaasu S. Gavarasana

Copyright © 2016 Vaasu S. Gavarasana
All rights reserved.

ISBN: 1537636421
ISBN 13: 9781537636429

To my wife, Leena Gavarasana,
who helped the many flowers in my life blossom

The views published in this book are my own and do not represent the intellectual property or opinion of any organization.

Contents

Introduction xi

Section 1 The What and Why of Digital Transformation 1
Chapter 1 Why Digital Transformation? 3
Chapter 2 What's the Difference between IT and Digital? 5
Chapter 3 Are Digital and Digital Marketing Different? 8
Chapter 4 Seven Mistakes that Derail Digital Transformation 11

Section 2 The Path to Digital Transformation · · · · · 17
Chapter 1 The Right Leader and Organization Structure · 19
Chapter 2 Change Philosophy · · · · · · · · · · · · · · · · · · · 22
Chapter 3 Plot Customer Path2Engagement · · · · · · · · 24
Chapter 4 Muster and Cluster · · · · · · · · · · · · · · · · · · · 27
Chapter 5 Mull and Cull · 28
Chapter 6 No Digital Lipstick for the Legacy Pig · · · · · 30
Chapter 7 The Churchillian Charge · · · · · · · · · · · · · · · 32
Chapter 8 The *Star Trek* Bridge · · · · · · · · · · · · · · · · · · 34

Introduction

Living is easy with eyes closed.

—JOHN LENNON

When electric power first appeared on the scene, people were suspicious. The promise of an uninterrupted supply of light and power was bewitching. People were suspicious of this witchcraft.

The invention of the electric light bulb threatened the oil monopoly. People discovered that, unlike firewood, electricity was easy to use, available during all seasons, and, most importantly, safer.

Electricity's quick win to light up homes also warmed people's hearts. Productivity improved, income went up, the rate of accidents fell, and quality of life at home improved dramatically. As people experienced the benefits of electric power, they were willing to embrace other applications. Over time it became agreeable to move away from oil to electric power.

Digital is experiencing the same transitory challenges that electric power faced in the early part of the nineteenth century. The important lesson to take away is that just like electric power, digital will prevail.

Digital transformation is not the regular train journey we all know. It's a long roller-coaster ride. It makes first timers dizzy, vomit, and then get scared. Fight this fear. Hold on to the handrail, scream out your lungs, and enjoy the ride. Believe me. It's worth it.

Section 1

The What and Why of Digital Transformation

Chapter 1

Why Digital Transformation?

In the beginning, business was simple. People who had surplus agricultural produce would exchange it with people who wanted to trade goods or services. We called it "bartering." This type of exchange was direct and instant, and the value was mutually beneficial. The advent of modern money and mass production changed this dynamic forever by altering the flow of commerce. Mass production, the child of the industrial revolution, created distance between the business and the person it served (from direct to indirect).

The chief benefit of bartering was the immediate unlocking of mutual value by direct interaction. Let's call this concept "Direct and Instant Delivery of Mutual Value," or DIDMV. We now have a great opportunity to once again embrace customer centricity by adopting digital transformation that delivers DIDMV.

Simply speaking, digital transformation is the process that delivers customer centricity by applying the principles of DIDMV. The application of DIDMV realigns the business around the customer journey, helping you create direct connections that deliver mutual and immediate value.

Chapter 2

What's the Difference between IT and Digital?

A 2014 report by Altimeter Group cites 54 percent of CMOs, 29 percent of CTOs/CIOs, and 15 percent of CDOs leading digital transformation. Because consumer Internet companies kicked off the digital revolution, it's easy to understand why CMOs stepped in to lead the charge. It's equally easy to understand how CTOs got involved, because computer-science engineers build most digital tools.

If CMOs own digital marketing and information technology (IT) owns technology, who owns digital? But first, what *is* digital, and how is it different from IT?

IT—or the term "information technology" in its modern sense—first appeared in a 1958 article published in the *Harvard Business Review*. Authors Harold J. Leavitt and Thomas L. Whisler commented that "the new technology does not yet have a single established name. We shall call it information technology (IT)." The definition consisted of three categories: techniques for processing; the application of statistical and mathematical methods to decision making; and the simulation of higher-order thinking through computer programs.

Wikipedia defines information technology (IT) as the application of computers and telecommunications equipment to store, retrieve, transmit, and manipulate data, often in the context of a business. In a simplified sense, IT is all about infrastructure that converts data to actionable information. Business leaders have long used IT to improve productivity, drive efficiency, and lower costs.

Because IT was involved in delivery of management information and efficiencies, it quickly became the backbone of all corporate functions. And eventually a new corporate function was born with its own C-level leader, the CTO/CIO.

IT became a critical business function. In this context, it's easy to understand why IT seeks perfection. It is deliberately thoughtful, thorough, and, as a result, slow to move. To preserve business momentum and avoid any downtime, IT infrastructure has to be robust and built to last.

Very often IT and digital are confused. This confusion is due to similar physical appearances. But deep inside, they differ widely in their philosophy.

I define "digital" as an always-on agile approach that is built on IT to deliver a direct and symbiotic relationship between the customer and the company using the Internet as the core channel.

The guiding principle for digital is not based on the perfection that IT seeks. A state of perfection assumes an ideal end state achieved by a specified end date, followed by acts of maintenance to preserve the state of perfection. This mind-set assumes that customer behavior evolves slowly and linearly and is sufficiently managed by upgrades and fixes.

However, while digital also embraces the philosophy of perfection, it defines it differently. Because digital is an approach, it seeks perfection through a series of progressive, agile acts that continuously seek harmony with the customer. Clearly, digital seeks external harmony, whereas IT seeks internal harmony.

Chapter 3

Are Digital and Digital Marketing Different?

Just like electricity in my introduction, digital has many applications, the most popular being digital marketing. "Digital" and "digital marketing" are often used interchangeably in conversations, as if they have the same meaning. This misconception is easy to understand and can be traced back to consumer technology companies like Yahoo, Google, and Facebook making digital popular.

In my perspective, digital has two main application areas, the first being the engagement of people—for example, employees, vendors, consumers, and customers. The second application area is internal business processes, with a goal to shorten and simplify all processes.

Digital Lipstick on a Legacy Pig !

I also strongly feel that the phrase "digital marketing" is a myopic take on marketing. It should be "marketing in and to a digital world" and not "digital marketing."

Marketing is undergoing its own transformation, which digital transformation is currently overshadowing. The rise of Internet of Things (IOT) devices will drive marketing transformation. Agile marketing based on data, currently in its infancy, will become the essential way that business operates.

Here are a few other changes we will see in marketing:

1. We will move away from "assumption data" to "live real-time data." Today assumption data largely influences marketing. These are assumptions we make based on past data. Live data will shape the future of marketing.
2. Marketing will shift from product propositions to consumer ecosystems. The aggregate value derived from the ecosystem will be far greater than Unique Selling Propositions (USP)
3. Fixed-period marketing campaigns will give way to always-on marketing. This is because people are always on. Are brands always on?
4. Top of mind (TOM) awareness as a metric will decline in importance and give way to new metrics, like share of connectedness and share of social chatter.

5. The upper-funnel spray-and-pray approach will decline as response rates decline. This is already happening. This will change the shape of the marketing funnel as we know it today.
6. Devices streaming live data will challenge marketing messages carrying product propositions and perceptions. If the messaging doesn't match the data, advertising will lose credibility.
7. In marketing communications, utility and entertainment content (UE) will trump unique selling proposition messaging (USP). Content marketing driven by UE is becoming the new advertising.
8. Brand personification, largely ignored today, will become more important. In a social world, a point of view is needed to engage in a conversation. The facelessness of brands will disappear.

Tip : Get a mannequin into the marketing room and play a 'brand persona' dress up game. Then brainstorm how that 'persona' would speak to different people (audiences).

Chapter 4

Seven Mistakes that Derail Digital Transformation

Christopher Columbus wasn't handed a map. But I am sure he wished for one. He probably would have reached India instead of the Americas. Despite failing to meet the objective, he was hailed a hero. All of us don't get lucky with our mistakes.

Here are seven mistakes I discovered in my own digital transformation voyage. I am sharing this with the hope of helping companies accomplish a smooth digital transformation.

Mistake 1: Uncommitted CEOs

Historically speaking, corporate transformations used a bottom-up approach to effect change. A lot of emphasis and action was placed on people buy in to the change. In this context, the role of the CEO was to evangelize, execute change management, and be patient with the marination process. Unfortunately, this approach doesn't work with digital transformation. There are several reasons (beyond the scope of this book) why this approach has consistently failed.

For digital transformation to be effective, the board and the chairperson have to demand action from the CEO and then bake digital Key Performance Indicators (KPIs) into the CEO's performance evaluation and bonus with a higher weight on action taken.

Does your CEO have digital KPIs?

Mistake 2A: Being Hijacked by Vanity Projects and Quick Wins

The spirit of a quick win is well placed. It plays a big role in creating trust and momentum in the company. But once a quick win is not a delivery milestone in a strategic project timeline, it's nothing but a distraction. It serves no purpose other than to create an illusion of progress. The quick win then sucks up valuable investment and resources, thus distracting from the bigger digital journey.

Tip: Advocate a series of small wins, which are part of a strategic road map.

Mistake 2B: Bling vs. the Iceberg

Who doesn't love a quick win that can be showcased? This is true for most business activities, but not for digital. Digital has two unique characteristics: it is outcome based, and it looks like an iceberg. You see only parts of it; the remaining big chunk is invisible.

In a world that loves bling, digital has a handicap. It's not easily visible and leads people to dismiss progress being made. Often projects get killed for the perceived lack of progress (despite regular update meetings).

Digital transformation needs a different viewing lens, and this is where CEOs can step in and evangelize the progress.

Tip: The correct way to check digital progress is to look for data, not the dress.

Mistake 3: To Be or Not to Be inside Marketing?

Digital transformation is not a subdiscipline of marketing. Marketing usually has a business-as-usual agenda. Placing digital transformation within marketing is like locking a tiger in a cage and then expecting to see great leaps. Digital transformation needs to be an independent function reporting directly to the CEO.

Organizations need to undertake two transformations. One is to embrace DIDMV (discussed earlier); the second is the transformation of the marketing function. Clive Sirkin, CMO of Kimberly-Clark, once said, "We don't believe in digital marketing. We believe in marketing in a digital world."

Tip: Make two new hires. Every company needs a chief digital officer (CDO). Hire a digital-savvy CMO (or train the old-school CMOs).

Mistake 4: Not Yet a Self-Driven Car!

Digital transformation needs a minimum viable team. Stakeholders across the organization are important partners in the transformation journey, but they are not substitutes for dedicated people tasked with transformation.

Mistake 5: The Paper Tiger Eats the Digital Cow for Lunch

Traditional projects need exhaustive documentation, especially IT projects. A digital project needs a one-pager with data KPIs for approval, not a hundred-page document. The lean canvas is a good example of a one-page document.

Digital is all about doing. Don't spend weeks and months creating a document. Instead spend that time creating a prototype and testing it.

Joi Ito of MIT Media Lab once said, "Deploy or die."

Mistake 6: No Dedicated Budget for Digital Transformation

IT and digital need their own budgets, as they are interdependent parts of a continuous value chain. Often digital budgets sit within IT and marketing, and the digital transformation function has no funding. This travesty is perhaps the single biggest detrimental factor to achieving digital transformation.

Mistake 7: Digital Transformation and Customer Centricity as Parallel Tracks

The disruptive consumer-facing technologies of the twenty-first century have revived the focus on customer centricity. However, companies often make the mistake of running digital transformation and customer centricity in parallel (with a few common stations along the way). As advocated in this book, the purpose of digital transformation is to deliver customer centricity by embracing DIDMV.

Having two parallel paths leads to rivalry for budgets and resources and creates friction.

Tip: If you already have two tracks, merge them. If you are starting afresh, adopt DIDMV.

I also want to clarify the use of the word "customer." I am using "customer" and "consumer" as words with the same meaning. I am not implying any B2B or B2C context.

The implementation of DIDMV flows from the principles of design thinking, which has its origins in artistic design but has since embraced a much-larger scope. Unfortunately, the label of "design thinking" gives people the impression that it has an art skew. I prefer "human-centric design." It's about bringing human empathy back into the business.

Section 2

The Path to Digital Transformation

Chapter 1

The Right Leader and Organization Structure

Nothing illustrates the impact of digital in our lives better than the TV series *Star Trek*. The show inspired many technological innovations we see today, starting with the mobile phone.

So who should lead digital transformation? Captain Kirk or Scotty? The answer is neither. The best candidate is Commander Spock, a leader with a perfect blend of EQ and IQ who makes decisions based on data.

Spock would have made a good chief marketing technologist, a hybrid role combining elements of the CMO and CIO. The emergence of a chief marketing technologist (*Harvard Business Review*, July 2014) is an interesting development in North America. But we are a long way off in finding this talent in sufficient numbers to lead digital transformation across Fortune 500 companies.

However, the current trend, to give the digital role to a marketing person, is a well-founded notion. The skill set of a marketer and the outcome of digital transformation are well aligned (customer centricity).

At most organizations, I notice digital transformational leaders reporting to the CMO. On the face of it, it looks logical unless you dig one layer down to discover an inherent flaw in this organizational design.

The digital marketing leader should report to the CMO. If the digital transformation leader reports to the CMO, then transformation will slow down, as it fights for its share of support with Business-As-Usual (BAU).

The natural instinct of marketing or any other function is to protect and preserve BAU and the evolutionary growth of the company. The BAU ethos will conflict with the transformational agenda, resulting in transformational paralysis.

The correct structure is to have an independent transformation function, reporting directly to the CEO. The

Digital Lipstick on a Legacy Pig !

CEO is the only leader responsible for the company's future, therefore attaining perfect alignment of strategic goals.

Before we close this point, I want to propose the creation of digital teams in every function. Just as marketing has digital marketing, there should be digital finance, digital distribution, digital sales, and so on. Eventually all functions should have a digital core. As the company transforms, the silo functions should disintegrate and appear as a series of experts spread across the customer journey.

Action

Create a new transformation function reporting directly to the CEO. This function needs budgetary and head-count allocation and, most critically, an unequivocal CEO mandate.

Chapter 2

Change Philosophy

Customer centricity is not a project. It is a culture. Embrace human-centric design.

Quality guru Joseph M. Juran (1988) popularized the concept of an internal customer. It became widely popular, gaining wide acceptance in the business world. This then led to the creation of the standard operating procedure for interdepartmental interaction. The logic was that achieving internal customer satisfaction would result in external customer satisfaction. Authors Tansuhaj, Randall, and McCullough (1991) supported this notion, arguing that service organizations that design products for internal customer satisfaction are better able to satisfy the needs of external customers.

Digital Lipstick on a Legacy Pig !

This concept found a perfect home in the modern corporation of the twentieth century, which had grown in departmental complexity with multiple layers of managers who often lived in their own wells. With everyone busy looking after each other, who was looking after the end paying customer?

In the digital era, we know this approach is no longer sustainable. I am proposing a paradigm change, where every function rids itself of the notion of the internal customer and related processes to directly focus and interact with the end customer.

Action
Every department needs a new mission (actions) statement focused on helping the customer. The ambition should be to deliver the customer journey in one click or one action away.

Chapter 3

Plot Customer Path2Engagement

Digital journeys designed on human behavior deliver real dollar value. A McKinsey study found that a telecommunications company executed faster sign-ups that increased customer satisfaction by 20 percent and reduced costs by 30 percent. A *Business Insider* report estimates that about $100 million of merchandise was ordered via same-day delivery in 2014, generating about $20 million in shipping fees. (The analysis covers just twenty US cities.)

A new generation of consumers are using a multitude of connected devices, resulting in multiple paths to engagement and purchase. At first glance, it appears that every customer has his or her own unique path. But that isn't the case, according to a McKinsey study that found there is a core consumer journey that covers 80 percent of the customer base. It's far more prudent to figure out this core journey rather than attempt to build a unique journey for every consumer. It's aspirational but not pragmatic.

For hard product categories (unlike soft product categories like education, travel, and financial services), there is no published data on what constitutes a core journey. However, we are seeing an emergence of three core models: click for delivery (old model), click and collect, and showrooming.

So how do you get started? I recommend plotting the customer journey from two points. One starts from the brand product awareness to payment and delivery. Why and how did that shampoo end up in the bathroom? Why and how did that insurance policy end up in your file at home?

The second investigation runs backward. The mapping starts at postpurchase at the customer's home and ends at the very start of the consumer journey (awareness). How did he or she know? Why did he or she buy? How did he or she pay?

The timing, location, duration, and intensity of each step should be measured. The objective is to discover moments of opportunity along the path to engagement and purchase.

The final step is to reconcile the two journeys. An analysis of the two journeys and associated data will help marketers discover actionable patterns in the engagement and purchase behavior.

Insight

Humans are creatures of habit. What might start as an erratic path eventually ends up in a pattern. Don't fall into the trap of creating multiple unique journeys for all the customers.

Action

To find profitable patterns, study all the microactions in the customer's forward journey from awareness to purchase and then the journey in reverse from purchase to awareness.

On a side note, microactions are the not the same as Google's micromoments.

Chapter 4

Muster and Cluster

The muster and cluster is the most important step in the implementation of digital transformation. You will progress through the following steps:

1. Draw up a muster of all activities of all the functions.
2. Separate all the activities into two clusters: one cluster of activities that directly interact with the end customer, and the second cluster of activities that interact with other functions inside the company.
3. Further bifurcate each cluster into two types of activities: activities done manually or IT-enabled activities.
4. List all the manual and IT activities within each cluster and then rank them on direct business impact, indirect-but-delivers business impact, reporting activity, and administrative activity.

Chapter 5

Mull and Cull

This step helps prioritize action. The transformation team, along with business stakeholders, must mull over the final list and then plan the culling of unnecessary activities (followed by retraining and reallocation of staff). The execution planning should prioritize all manual activities that have direct customer contact with high business impact.

The second priority is to mull over all indirect manual activities. Examine each manual activity that is routed through another internal function before reaching the end customer. Please question this interdependency. Does the activity need a transit stop via another department? What value is the second department (transit stop) adding to the process before touching the customer? Can the first

Digital Lipstick on a Legacy Pig !

department do this directly? If yes, what steps need to be added digitally to make a path straight to the customer?

All reporting and administrative activities must be examined for their utility to the end customer. Most companies blindly follow standard operating procedures and never pause to ask why.

Finally, an audit across the company is important to uncover duplicate activities—that is, two different functions/departments doing the same activity. You will be surprised at the number of duplicate activities that come out of the closet in a silo-structured, geographically dispersed large corporation. I think you have already guessed the follow-up action.

Chapter 6

No Digital Lipstick for the Legacy Pig

Would you take an old cassette tape player and try to convert it to a smartphone that streams music? Or would you rather place it on your mantelpiece and buy a new smartphone?

Most legacy corporate IT systems have made money for their companies. They are depreciated and outdated assets. Yet I find many companies trying to put digital lipstick on their legacy systems. I recommend starving them of new and repeat business, eventually leading to their operational obsolescence and retirement.

Digital Lipstick on a Legacy Pig !

Action

Build a new platform, and feed all new customer actions into this new platform. All renewals and repeat business should be fed into the new system. As the new platform expands, the legacy platform will shrink and become irrelevant to the business.

Building new platforms and creating "Application Programming Interfaces" (APIs) must go hand in hand. API is not a downstream activity. Companies must include APIs in their planning, before building any IT or digital platforms.

Chapter 7

The Churchillian Charge

Winston Churchill, a great communicator, could rouse an entire nation with his eloquent speeches. Equally important were his visits to the front lines, where he would fire up soldiers with his talks.

A mistake most companies make is to restrict digital transformation updates to the ranks of the digital steering committee and the board. No one else in the company gets to know what's happening on a regular basis.

This is an opportunity to drive culture change. Customer centricity is not a project with regular reporting. It's a culture. It needs a guru, not a project manager! Where is your Churchill?

Action

Ideally the CEO should take up the Churchillian charge. But if you have a CEO who isn't articulate, there is no harm assigning this responsibility to a good speaker within the company.

Chapter 8

The *Star Trek* Bridge

"We cannot manage what we cannot measure." I am equally excited and puzzled to see digital social-listening centers springing up with a lot of fanfare. I agree this is important for marketing (and to show off digital progress to staff and visitors). But where is the equivalent for the business?

Where is the heads-up display (HUD) for the captain of the ship? Remember the *Star Trek* bridge? We see captain Kirk surrounded by officers and screens streaming information for decision making.

Digital Lipstick on a Legacy Pig !

Action

Create a comprehensive digital command center with a bank of screens streaming data for decision making. This is important, both for functional and drama value.

This center should be the office of the C suite. The CEO with all his C-level colleagues should sit together in a *Star Trek* kind of configuration, to boldly go where no company has gone before.

No CEO wants a Kodak or a Nokia situation. Digital transformation is a great opportunity for company leaders to deliver DIDMV and drive a customer-centric culture.

An opportunity to set course for a sustainable and profitable future. To boldly go where no enterprise has gone before. As Spock would say, "Live long, and prosper." RIP, Leonard Nimoy.

www.ingramcontent.com/pod-product-compliance
Lightning Source LLC
Chambersburg PA
CBHW071839200526
45169CB00020B/1948